Time

by Suki Sataka
illustrated by Ana Ochoa

 HOUGHTON MIFFLIN   BOSTON

Copyright © by Houghton Mifflin Company. All rights reserved.

No part of this work may be reproduced or transmitted in any form or by any means, electronic or mechanical, including photocopying or recording, or by any information storage or retrieval system without the prior written permission of Houghton Mifflin Company unless such copying is expressly permitted by federal copyright law. Address inquiries to School Permissions, Houghton Mifflin Company, 222 Berkeley Street, Boston, MA 02116.

Printed in China

ISBN 10: 0-618-88669-9
ISBN 13: 978-0-618-88669-2

8 9 10 11 0940 17 16 15 14
4500460323

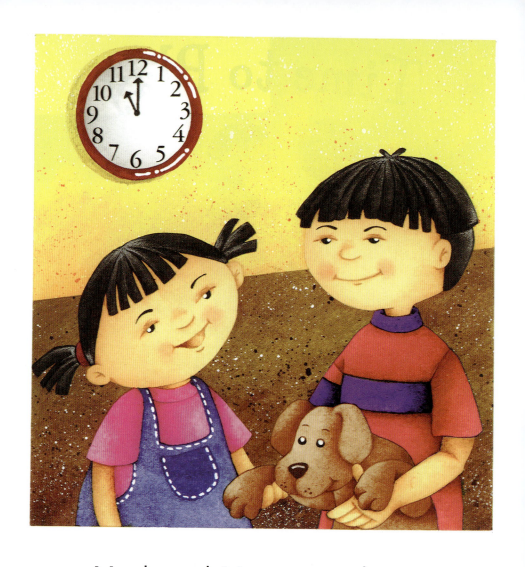

Mark and Mary can play after they eat lunch. Lunch is at 12 o'clock.

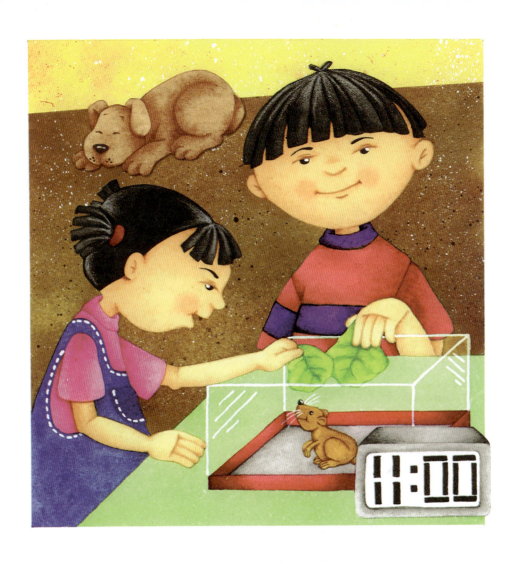

Mary and Mark feed Fuzzy. Their pets always eat an hour before they do.

What time does Fuzzy eat?

Mary feeds her bird.
Chirpo eats a half hour before Mark and Mary.

Did Mary feed her bird before or after feeding Fuzzy?

Bubbles is hungry, too.
Mark feeds his fish a half
hour before lunch.

What time is it?

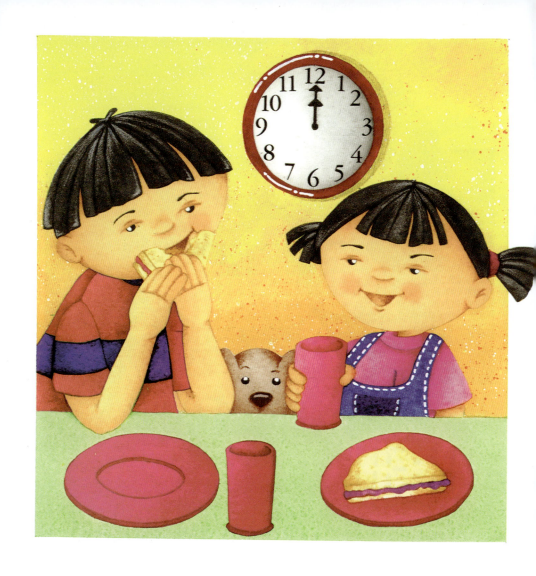

Finally, Mark and Mary eat lunch.

What time is it now?

Playtime!

Responding

Vocabulary

A Clock and a Clock

Draw

Look at pages 4 and 5. Draw the two clocks you see.

Tell About

Compare and Contrast Look at the clocks on pages 4 and 5. Tell how the clocks are different. Tell what time each clock shows. Tell how the clocks are alike.

Write

Look at pages 4 and 5. Write the time each clock shows.